Envisage YOUR Beauty Business

The Ultimate Guide For Setting Up and Running A Successful Salon From Home

Jo McKenzie

First published by Busybird Publishing 2018
Copyright © 2018 Jo McKenzie

ISBN
Print: 978-1-925692-70-9
Ebook: 978-1-925692-71-6

Jo McKenzie has asserted her right under the Copyright, Designs and Patents Act 1988 to be identified as the author of this work. The information in this book is based on the author's experiences and opinions. The publisher specifically disclaims responsibility for any adverse consequences, which may result from use of the information contained herein. Permission to use information has been sought by the author. Any breaches will be rectified in further editions of the book.

All rights reserved. No part of this publication may be reproduced, stored in or introduced into a retrieval system, or transmitted in any form, or by any means (electronic, mechanical, photocopying, recording or otherwise) without the prior written permission of the author. Any person who does any unauthorised act in relation to this publication may be liable to criminal prosecution and civil claims for damages. Enquiries should be made through the publisher.

Cover image: Kev Howlett
Cover design: Busybird Publishing
Layout and typesetting: Busybird Publishing

Busybird Publishing
2/118 Para Road
Montmorency, Victoria
Australia 3094
www.busybird.com.au

DISCLAIMER
This is not intended to be a financial planning book. All statistics and figures are correct at the time of publication but will not suit all situations. It is highly recommended that legal, financial and taxation advice is sought for your own situation. There is no substitute for professional advice when dealing with the best way to set up your business and the author and publisher disclaim any responsibility for the outcomes associated with action taken in relation to the contents of this book. Due diligence is key for your own peace of mind.

Testimonials

Jo is a true professional … focused, driven, and dedicated to delivering the absolute best of care and services for her clients. She has an amazing skill set, combined with in-depth knowledge of the beauty industry. These attributes, along with her dedication to keeping up with the latest research, trends, and techniques have enabled her to run a very successful home-based beauty business for almost twenty years.

This book is an absolute must-read for anyone in the market for the guidance and expertise of an industry veteran. It is the ultimate guide that saves time and money for anyone setting up their own home-based beauty salon.

Karen Cormack
Owner, Integrity Online – Websites & Digital Marketing Services, www.integrityonline.com.au

It has been an absolute pleasure to be part of Jo McKenzie's journey. I believe her passion, drive, and determination, along with her ability to be flexible and embrace change, have ensured her success and longevity in the beauty industry. She seeks support when needed and turns her challenges into opportunities. If you're wanting to start your business and build it into a successful and rewarding career at whichever level works for you, take the time to read ... it will not only guide you through step by step, but also support you through emotionally when the unexpected comes up.

Debra Zabenko
Life Fulfilment Coaching & Hypnotherapy

I am delighted to say I have been a client of Jo's for over ten years and I love the salon environment she has created. It feels discreet and private with a very personal touch while still offering a professional level of service. Jo's friendly manner, combined with her knowledge of the treatments and products that are used, is so informative and every cosmetic procedure is always well explained.

Jo is so passionate about her work and is always updated with the latest cosmetic techniques. I would highly recommend Jo to anyone seeking advice for their skin and beauty needs.

Alba Veronese
Senior Leader, Silk Oil of Morocco

I have been lucky enough to have spent the last ten years as Jo's client at "Envisage Beauty". The comments I have had from people in general about the great condition of my skin is because of the knowledge, professionalism and passion of Jo. Her salon is so professional but also has a very relaxed atmosphere. Jo always makes me feel so welcomed and important. I wouldn't dream of going elsewhere as I truly don't believe that I would receive any better or warmer treatment.

Tania Hutchins
Accounts Receivable Clerk

Jo's salon has a friendly but professional atmosphere. Upon arrival, it is clearly signposted and customer parking is provided. There is a comfortable waiting area with product displays and reading materials. Jo discusses treatments and products regularly and attends various training sessions. She is clearly up to date with her knowledge and skills. Her salon is very relaxing and Jo is always well presented in her uniform. Communication is great, with Jo responding to texts or calls within a short time frame. I have been a client for about four years and look forward to my visits without having to deal with big car parks or noisy salons at major shopping centres!

Lyn Regan
Retired School Principal

Dedication

To my two beautiful children, James and Alana, who have not only been the focus of my world but my strongest motivation.

To my parents, thank you for believing in me and supporting my dream all those years ago.

To my amazing partner, Zac, whose love, encouragement, and support gives me the confidence to take a chance and follow my heart.

Contents

1. Introduction	3
2. Getting Started	11
3. Money Matters	21
4. Set Up For Success	29
5. Work Smarter, Not Harder!	39
6. Get Equipped	51
7. Believe In Your Brand	61
8. Stop Selling, Start Helping	69
9. My Secret Planning Tips for Success	91
Afterword	101
Acknowledgements	103
About The Author	105
Offers	107
Bonus Interview with Lourbuen Perez-Vergamalis	109
Bonus Interview with Tania De Vincentis	115

It's a beautiful thing when a career and a passion come together

1
Introduction

After many years of being asked about how I have run a successful clinic from home for over sixteen years, I decided to write this book to share my key strategies and secrets. My goal is to help others realise their dream of starting their own business to enjoy the flexibility and benefits of working from home without compromising on professionalism.

From my experience, a home-based clinic can be very successful and profitable. If the salon owner has the right information and expertise to create a professional environment, there is a considerable market for clients who prefer this more personal setting.

Why I opened my salon from home

In 2002 my circumstances changed in my personal life and I found myself a single mum with no job, no family nearby, and two small children under five to take care of. This was not part of the plan, or the path I thought I would find myself taking.

However, I have learnt that, as women and as mums, we are more resilient and resourceful than we could ever imagine. I had to find a way to support myself and my children that provided a good source of income but also allowed plenty of flexibility. I also needed to build my confidence and self-esteem, and to focus on something positive after the breakdown of my marriage.

My career in the beauty business started in my early 20s when I signed up as a part-time skincare consultant for a direct selling company. I began doing party plans, teaching groups of ladies how to care for their skin and apply make-up. I loved sharing my knowledge and working with women, and I quickly realised my passion for the beauty industry. I was awarded the title of Queen of Sales and Queen of Recruiting in my first year, which also reinforced that I had found my calling. I decided to leave my full-time job after seven years in the tourism industry, move to Melbourne from the country town I grew up in, and pursue my beauty career.

I studied full time and obtained my Diploma of Beauty Therapy at the Ella Baché Academy. I was offered a job at a leading salon in Melbourne, where I worked for the next seven years. I was fortunate to learn from someone who was well respected in the industry and a very good businesswoman. Having moved from the country and not knowing anyone in Melbourne, the girls I worked with became my "Melbourne family", and I have very fond memories of my time there.

1. Introduction

After I was married and had my children, I continued to work on and off in the beauty industry and also helped out in my husband's real estate business.

When my marriage ended, I realised I needed to make some serious decisions about my career options. It had always been my intention to work for myself with my own business at some point. I decided this was my moment of truth and I wanted to prove to myself that I could do this. I started to look at my options. Renting a shop and opening a salon seemed too daunting and too inflexible given my current situation. I decided the best option was to open my clinic from home, build the business up for a couple of years, and then move to a larger salon premises.

Fast forward sixteen years, I still operate my clinic from home and wouldn't have it any other way. My home based beauty business has allowed me the financial security and flexibility to be able to enjoy a good lifestyle, lovely home, family holidays, and to be able to send my children to the school of our choice.

One million Australians run a business from home

Why not you?

Would you like more time for yourself?

Would you like flexible working hours to work around your family?

Are you tired of working for someone else and seeing the profits of your hard work going to them?

Have you dreamed of owning your own business and being your own boss?

There are many, many benefits to operating a professional salon from your home environment. If you have ever dreamed of being your own boss and having your own salon, but the thought of the financial and time commitments necessary are just too overwhelming, then this book is for you.

If you are afraid to take the first step on your own, I am here to take it with you. Here is your step-by-step guide to getting started on your way to working for yourself, running your own professional salon whilst enjoying the flexibility and benefits of working from home, and having more time, money and energy to spend with your family.

I read that a commuter can spend, on average, 38 hours a year stuck in traffic! Imagine having that much extra time to fit in the other things you would rather do. As well as saving time, you save on fuel, parking and public transport costs. There are also financial benefits when you work from home such as being able to claim a portion of your home living expenses on tax.

This book is about sharing what I have learnt to help you fast track your business for success. I will teach you how to correctly set up a professional salon business from home: the necessary steps, proven formulas, and strategies I have used to ensure success and longevity in this business.

If you already work from home or have a small salon, many of the strategies and ideas in this book can be used for inspiration and motivation, and to hopefully breathe new life into your business.

Start small and dream big.

Best wishes for every success.

Love,

Jo

XXXXX

And suddenly you just know ... it's time to start something new and trust the magic of beginnings.

– Meister Eckhardt

If you want something you've never had, you must be willing to do something you've never done

2
Getting Started

The power of positivity

Once I had made the decision to open my salon from home, I remembered making a conscious effort to focus on staying positive and excited rather than allowing negative thoughts or doubts creep in. I was also careful who I told about my upcoming venture as I didn't want other peoples' fears to knock my confidence. Well meaning family members or close friends can sometimes say things out of concern, but these thoughts can niggle away at you and I couldn't afford to entertain that kind of mindset. A close friend said to me "Aren't you worried? What if it doesn't work?" My reply was, "It has to work. There's no other option". That was the attitude

I adopted. I knew I would find a way, or make one. I was determined to succeed and that meant taking a leap of faith, staying open minded, and being willing to adjust my approach when needed.

I love Dr Phil's quote, "Life rewards action". For me, that meant just keep doing small steps to building your business, and those steps and actions will start to gather momentum. Nothing happens without taking some form of action.

Speaking of action, before we go any further with planning, there are some things we need to consider. I have compiled a list to help you determine the potential capacity of your home to cater for your home business. This is a guide only to help point out what you may need to modify to suit your particular situation.

Your Checklist:

Your room:
- ☐ Do you have a suitable room to conduct your salon from?
- ☐ Is it located at the front of the house, offering easy access, or will clients need to walk through the rest of your house?
- ☐ Are toilet/hand washing facilities close by?
- ☐ Do you have a room adjacent or close by to use as your waiting area when client appointments overlap? Is there room for seating, a coffee table, brochures, etc.?
- ☐ Does your room have heating during winter and cooling during summer, or do you need to have these installed?

2. Getting Started

- ☐ Does your room have a hard surface on the floor, such as tiles or floorboards? (Carpet is not suitable for health reasons)
- ☐ Does your room have a sink? If not, is the plumbing easily accessible for installation?
- ☐ If you plan on having a landline for your business, does your room have a phone line already installed? If not, can this be easily installed? Be aware that some EFTPOS machines require a phone line. Another option is to use your mobile phone and a portable payment facility.
- ☐ Does your room have access to power and/or do you need an electrician to install more power outlets for your equipment, etc.?
- ☐ Is there sufficient lighting in the room? Is it dimmable to offer a variety of lighting options? It is good to have low lighting for relaxation treatments, while much stronger task lighting is required for other treatments.

Contact your local council:

Ask your local council for their guidelines about home salons. Council regulations change according to your state and jurisdiction.

They may suggest you come in and meet with a council officer, or they may send someone out to advise you of any zoning regulations and whether any special permits are required. Generally no special permits are required if the building you are working from is your place of residence.

Council registration:

You need to register your business with your local council who will organise your registration for the Public Health and Wellbeing Act. An officer from the council may come out to help you with planning, which I strongly advise, as you want to know what the regulations are before you start preparing your room. It is best to get the right advice upfront, rather than spending money on your salon only to find it doesn't meet council guidelines.

It is likely that you may need to consider some plumbing modifications in your room depending on what treatments you plan to offer. I would suggest installing a sink or vanity in the room, even if it is not initially necessary.

Otherwise, you may be limited in the future as to what treatments you can offer. A hands-free tap can also be a requirement for some treatments, so it is best to have your room set up correctly upfront rather than having to do additional renovations or modifications later.

Your council inspector will also advise on the management of clinical waste and how to safely dispose of it. This is very important for the safety of yourself, your clients, and your family.

Download a copy of the "Health guidelines for personal care and body art industries" for all the industry specific requirements for beauty therapy procedures. It is a good idea to be familiar with these requirements prior to making contact with council. It is available at:

https://www2.health.vic.gov.au/public-health/infectious-diseases/personal-care-body-art-industries

Car parking:

- ☐ Do you have enough parking spaces outside for clients?
- ☐ Can you accommodate more than one car at a time when appointments overlap?
- ☐ Do you have room to create more parking space?
- ☐ Are your neighbours affected by clients parking or driving in your street?
- ☐ Do you need to talk to your neighbours?
- ☐ Are there any council regulations or restrictions?

I redesigned my front garden to allow for car parking. I have signs which show clients exactly where to park, which saves time and confusion when new clients visit and also ensures they are not parking in my neighbours' spaces.

Keep the neighbours on your side:

Think about when you should tell your neighbours about your planned venture. They may not appreciate it if they hear it from someone else first. I would suggest that once you know you have met all council criteria, think about going to see them or printing up a notice as a goodwill gesture. Be positive in your approach and reassure them that disruptions will be minimal and that you are open to discussing any problems. You could let them know that you would love for them to attend your opening celebrations and, as a thank you for their co-operation and support, you will offer special deals and discounts for neighbours and friends.

I threw a launch party for my salon and invited my neighbours so they felt part of it from the beginning. I always looked after them with "mates rates" and made sure I invited them to salon special events. Giving free samples or treatments from time to time helps to maintain a good relationship with your neighbours on an ongoing basis.

Other safety factors:
- ☐ Are your smoke detectors installed and fully functioning?
- ☐ Is a fire extinguisher present? If not, I would strongly suggest purchasing one and storing it somewhere close by where it is easily accessible.

Office area:

Do you wish to have a separate area set aside as your office?

You may be able to claim a portion of your home expenses if you run your salon and your office from home. It may also be possible to claim a portion of your mortgage interest, rates,

2. Getting Started

heating, phone and internet, electricity, water, cleaning, etc. This is where you need to talk to your accountant to find out what you can claim. Keep all receipts in case the Australian Taxation Office (ATO) performs an audit on your business. Audits are performed at random and you must keep records to satisfy the ATO.

Note:
It is not absolutely necessary to have a separate office area if space does not permit.

Whenever you see a successful business, someone once made a courageous decision

3
Money Matters

You will need to decide upon how much money you need to start up and run your business, and how you are going to fund it.

It is essential to do at least a basic business plan to have some direction and an idea of your short, medium and long-term goals for your business.

I would strongly advise getting some professional advice from an experienced business advisor such as a bank manager or accountant.

The Australian Securities and Investments Commission

(ASIC) have some helpful mobile apps you can download to calculate and manage your finances. Take a look at the ASIC's MoneySmart First Business app. It contains some simple budget templates, which you can use to track and estimate your set up and running costs, as well as many other helpful tools and information.

The www.business.gov.au website also offers some helpful advice about starting a business and in particular some information specifically related to home based businesses.

Local councils often run free courses for small businesses with relevant topics such as setting up your business or tips for marketing. It is worthwhile to consider attending one of these courses as they can provide lots of helpful contacts and information, and it's also a great opportunity to network with local people.

Once you have done your research into how much you require to start your business, it's time to decide how you are going to fund it.

Here are some suggestions:

Borrow money
Family or friends may be willing to put some money into your business upfront and help you get started. My advice is to have an agreement in writing that states the amount of money you have borrowed, any terms and conditions or interest agreed on, and very importantly, the date you agree to pay it back by. You may wish to repay the money in regular instalments, which is probably a better option than paying in a lump sum at the end.

You can also make an arrangement to repay all or some of the amount with salon treatments or products.

Bank loan

I would start with the bank you have the best relationship with. Approach your current bank(s) first for advice on what your borrowing capacity is, as they already have your history. They may require copies of tax returns and other documentation, so be prepared and check what you need to take for your meeting before you go. Once you know what is required and what they can offer, you may wish to approach a few different banks or money lending organisations, and then decide on the most suitable option.

Credit card

Apply for a credit card to use for your business, but you will need to be very disciplined and pay off each month before the due date or high interest rates apply. It is not advisable to start your business with a credit card if you can't afford to pay the balance off in the first month, because the interest rates are very high (usually around 20%). However, you will need a credit card for your business and it may be worthwhile looking into a business credit card that offers a rewards program. These can provide great rewards for yourself or your family without costing you anything.

I use a MasterCard and an American Express card for my business which gives me flexibility, great rewards programs, extra credit, and also a backup if one card fails for any reason.

Some tips to save money and keep your cash flowing:

Trading accounts

Always see if your suppliers are willing to give you an account. This means they will supply you with your products upfront and you agree to make payment at a later date, usually within 30 days. If you then pay your account by credit card, this gives you another possible 30-45 days until the credit card is due. This gives you the opportunity to sell your stock BEFORE you pay for it!

Lease agreement

You may wish to look into leasing your equipment over a certain period of time and paying it off. This is a good option as it doesn't tie up too much of your cash flow in one hit. You may have the option to own it outright at the end or upgrade to a newer model, which allows you to offer the most up to date technology.

(We will look at the leasing options in more detail in Chapter 5.)

Quotes for trades

When you are setting up your salon, you may need to enlist the help of some qualified tradespeople. There are some great online sites such as www.homeimprovementpages.com.au where you can invite qualified tradespeople in your area to provide quotes for your job. There are reviews you can read about each individual, and they must have the appropriate, up to date registrations. You can save money by shopping around, comparing quotes, and then choosing the most suitable person for the job. Remember, it's not always wise to choose the cheapest option. Trust your instincts and go for someone you feel is reliable and trustworthy.

Swap skills

Reduce your costs by offering to swap business skills. For example, you may have a friend who is a painter or tradesperson who can help with the fit out of your salon. Ask if they would be happy to do a swap for treatments, products or gift vouchers which they can use or give to family and friends. Be aware that you can offer to swap services for all sorts of things, especially when you are dealing with women.

*Stop calling it a dream.
It's time to plan.*

4
Set Up For Success

Step 1: It's all in the name

It's time to think about your business's name. You may already have one in mind, or have a brainstorming session and then run your ideas past family and friends for second opinions.

When I was trying to decide on the name for my salon, I invited a friend over who was starting a new website design business at the same time. I hadn't seen her for quite a while, so as well as our business agendas, we also had quite a bit of catching up to do on a personal level. The intention was to brainstorm together and help each other come up with some great options for our business names. The mistake we made was to open a bottle of wine. At the end of the night, we were convinced that we had come up with some brilliant options. However, the next day – minus the wine – they were terrible! We had a good laugh, and decided that the next time we worked together, we would stick to coffee.

I finally found the perfect name by just coming up with words, looking up their meanings, and trying to find something that resonated with me or meant something to me personally, but would also have appeal to my female market. I decided on "Envisage Professional Skincare Clinic", which I have since shortened to "Envisage Beauty". To envisage means to imagine something that hasn't happened yet, a vision for the future, to look in the face of. I felt this was perfect for me, as starting my own business was my vision, and also my work involves looking into faces.

Step 2: Make it legal

In order to register a business name you must have an Australian Business Number (ABN) or have applied for an ABN at the Australian Business Register (ABR). To do this, go to https://abr.gov.au.

It's worth talking to your accountant first to decide how you will structure your business, because when you register it, you need to know if you will be a sole trader, partnership, family trust or company. It is most likely that you will be a sole trader (unless you are working with someone else in your business) but it's still wise to understand your options. The way you structure your business will also have some bearing on any other assets you may have, so get advice.

Step 3: Register

Once you have decided on your name, go online to the ASIC website at www.asic.gov.au to check the availability of your proposed name. Be prepared to modify or have a few variations ready in case the name you want is already taken. The next step is to go ahead and register your business name. Go to ASIC Connect button on the Homepage, create an account, and then follow the steps to register. It costs $35 per year or $82 for three years to register a business. Your business name is not registered until your payment is received, so check that your payment goes through correctly and a receipt is issued. Print all receipts off and keep them as these expenses are all tax deductible. Make sure you are on the official ASIC website and not a third party website who registers the name on your behalf. You can get caught out with one of these websites, which charge extra to go through them when it is completely unnecessary.

Step 4: Accounting

You will need to decide how you are going to keep your business records. There are some great apps and programs if you choose to record the information online yourself. Have a look at QuickBooks, MYOB and Xero accounting software. If you want to use a cloud-based program, which is totally portable and compatible with your smartphone, tablet and other devices, these softwares can be very convenient. I would strongly suggest getting a bookkeeper, at least to help with your initial set up. You can choose whether you have the time to manage by yourself and then hand over to an accountant once a year for your tax return, or whether you prefer having a bookkeeper to manage your books for you all year round. The fees are tax deductible, or perhaps she/he may be happy to do a swap for services in the salon. Whichever you decide, you must be diligent with your record keeping as it is a legal requirement by the ATO.

> **Note:**
> The ATO advises that if a new business is likely to exceed $75,000 or more in its first year, you need to register for Good and Services Tax (GST).

Step 5: Payment tools

You will need to decide on how you are going to receive payment from your clients. I use an EFTPOS/credit card terminal from the Commonwealth Bank which costs around $16 per month plus credit card fees. I suggest you contact a few banks to see what rates they offer. There are other instant payment options available now and some banks offer an app for merchants that you can type the card details into and process payments instantly on your smartphone or tablet.

PayPal is worth setting up as well especially if you would like to add a shopping cart to your website. It is also a secure way to pay for supplies you need for your business. Link it to your credit card so you still get the benefit of interest-free terms.

Step 6: Insurance

You will need to take out separate insurance for your beauty business. Home and contents insurance is not appropriate cover for your business. I find insurance companies who specialise in beauty insurance are usually best, and you can find a number of these companies simply by googling them and getting some quotes. I am currently using Arthur J. Gallagher. & Co. You could also contact The Sparrow Group (www.thesparrowgroup.com.au) for a quotation.

I suggest you consider the following types of insurances:

- **Public Liability**: Protects against damages from a claim for personal injury or property damage that occurs as a result of business related activities.
- **Professional Indemnity:** Protection against financial losses for any legal action taken against you for services or advice provided.
- **Business Insurance:** To protect your business against material damage due to an unexpected event like fire, storm, theft, accidental damage, or financial loss due to an insurable event (business interruption).
- **Personal Accident and Illness:** Covers loss of income in the event that you suffer injury or illness and can't perform your usual work and earn income.

Step 7: Qualifications

Is your training complete and do you have the necessary certificates to verify your qualifications? I would suggest that the minimum qualification you need to run your own salon is a Diploma of Beauty Therapy, so make sure this is up to date or, if needed, take steps to complete this either online or part-time.

In most cases, you will need this base qualification before you can train in any of the more advanced skin therapies, such as skin needling, chemical peels and Intense Pulse Light (IPL)/laser treatments. It can also be a requirement for insurance purposes that you have the correct qualifications.

Step 8: Build a website

At this point, you may wish to start thinking about setting up your website. You could engage a professional to help, or if you are trying to keep costs down you can do it yourself or even hire a university student who is studying web design, marketing or IT. It is a good idea to have a website to attract new clients to your business, however this is something you could develop once the business is up and running.

You need to also register a domain name if you are going to have a business website. If you don't register your domain name, someone else could make a business using your name. For more information visit www.auDA.com.au (.au Domain Administration Ltd).

Step 9: Image

Now that you have your name, you need to think about your branding. The first step is to decide on your logo. There are many online companies who can design a logo for you to suit any budget. You need to have an idea of the style of your business and then reflect this in your logo. Do you want the look and feel of your business to be feminine and pretty to appeal to your female clients, or be simple and streamlined to give a more clinical/medical feel? These are questions to consider about your business so that the mood and feel of your business follows through consistently.

What sort of clients do you want to attract? Who is your ideal client? Your branding needs to appeal to this person.

(We will cover this in more detail in Chapter 7.)

4. Set Up For Success

Step 10: Promotion

Social media – decide which options you would like to use to market your business and set these up. It's about working out where your ideal client hangs out digitally. Popular platforms at the moment include Facebook, Instagram and Twitter, but do your homework and see what you are most comfortable with.

Sometimes it's a matter of testing what works best for you initially. I have included some suggestions for you to try a little later in the marketing section (Chapter 8). Enlist the help of family and friends and ask them to share your posts and invite people to join your page(s) and profile(s). I would suggest joining LinkedIn as well, as you can network with other professionals and it is another opportunity to showcase what you do.

Step 11: A picture speaks a thousand words!

It is a good idea to have some good shots of yourself and the salon to use for your marketing. You may opt to hire someone to take some professional shots of you, or you may know someone who can do these for you. Take a variety of shots, such as of you performing treatments, your room, and your products. If you don't have your salon ready yet, then get a good headshot of yourself, which you can use for your newsletters, brochures, blogs, and other promotional materials.

Ensure you and your salon look professional, and set up the salon so that it looks inviting for potential clients. Make sure you look like someone who your clients would take advice from about their skin and beauty needs. Your hair needs to be styled or tied up, make-up perfectly polished, and your outfit should look impeccable.

Step 12: Dress for success

Consider a uniform to wear in the salon. These make dressing for work days so much easier, and always look smart and professional. Stores like Target have great quality black pants, and you can shop around for smart tops and have them embroidered with your logo, or you can purchase from a salon uniform supplier. Take a look at Spring Spa Wear (www.springspawear.com.au).

Step 13: Looking for signs

I would suggest having some signage made to promote your business. I have a sign out the front of my home, which helps to advertise my business and lets new clients know they have the right place. It only needs to contain your salon name and phone number, but you could also add your website address if appropriate.

Consistent action creates consistent results

5

Work Smarter, Not Harder!

Choosing your treatment menu

Now is the time to decide what treatments you would like to offer.

Questions to ask yourself:

- What treatments do I enjoy doing?
- What am I good at?
- Which treatments are more profitable and offer the most return for my time?

- Which treatments are in demand?
- Are there treatments I could offer that no one else in this area is doing?

> **My Tip**
> Find a point of difference that you offer or specialise in.

There is no point setting up and offering the exact same treatments and products as other salons already established in your location. It is much smarter to do some research and offer something different. This also gives you the opportunity to network with other salons and see if they are open to working together to refer clients to each other and support each other's businesses, rather than viewing each other as competition.

Calculate costs

Now that you have some ideas about the treatments you may wish to offer, it's time to calculate how much it will cost to perform each treatment, and how much you can charge to give you a bottom line, and estimate which treatments will be more profitable. A body massage, for example, uses very little product, so most of the money taken from this is profit. It is, however, labour intensive, and you wouldn't want to be performing massages all day as this is very hard on your body. There is also very little opportunity to up-sell home care products with this treatment.

A facial treatment on the other hand would require more product, and possibly the use of equipment to perform, but can be done in less time. Also, if you do your job correctly and

5. Work Smarter, Not Harder!

educate your clients, most of them will purchase recommended home care products from you. I haven't included this into the cost figures below, but the potential for your retail add-on is an important consideration.

On page 42 (overleaf), look at some potential figures comparing treatment costings. You'll be able to see that the more advanced treatments using equipment or specialised skills offer much more profit in the long term. However, there is the cost of your equipment purchase or repayments to take into consideration, as well as possible training and qualification expenses.

On page 43, look at how much it may cost to purchase some equipment to enable you to offer the more advanced skin treatments.

Let's say, for example, you wanted to purchase a Hydro Dermabrasion machine for $8,000 and a skin-needling pen for $2,000. You would need to finance $10,000 which you could take out over a period of five years. Your repayments would be approximately $57 per week, or around $245 per month. You could cover this with just one to two treatments per week and the rest would go towards profit for your business. You can also claim 100% of the repayment amount as a tax deduction.

With the widespread usage of social media and Google, clients are much more educated and they are seeking treatments that offer results. They are more savvy in their choices and don't want to pay for something they can do by themselves at home with their own products. That is why I have found treatments using equipment seem to be favoured by clients these days. They are happy to pay more for these, as they understand they are getting advanced treatments using the latest technology which will deliver results they cannot achieve themselves.

Treatment Costing Chart

Treatment	Price	Less expenses	Time	Net cost	Profit/ hour
Massage	$75	$5	60 minutes	$70	$70
Full Leg Wax	$50	$10	30 minutes	$40	$80
Relaxation Facial	$120	$30	60 minutes	$90	$90
Chemical Peel	$130	$20	30 minutes	$110	$220
Microdermabrasion/Sonophoresis	$150	$20	30 minutes	$130	$260
Cosmetic Tattoo Eyebrows (2 sessions included)	$600	$15	150 minutes	$585	$234
Skin Needling (CIT) with recovery vitamin mask	$350	$50	30 minutes	$300	$600
IPL – Full Face Pigmentation/Skin Rejuvenation	$300	$15	30 minutes	$285	$570

5. Work Smarter, Not Harder!

Repayment Structure Guide

Amount (Exc. GST)	Term	Weekly repayment (Approx)	Monthly repayment (Approx)
$10,000	60 Months	$57	$245
$15,000	60 Months	$86	$368
$20,000	60 Months	$114	$490
$25,000	60 Months	$143	$613
$30,000	60 Months	$186	$804
$35,000	60 Months	$217	$937
$40,000	60 Months	$247	$1,071
$45,000	60 Months	$278	$1,204
$50,000	60 Months	$309	$1,337
$55,000	60 Months	$340	$1,471
$60,000	60 Months	$371	$1,605
$65,000	60 Months	$402	$1,738
$70,000	60 Months	$431	$1,872
$75,000	60 Months	$463	$2,006
$80,000	60 Months	$494	$2,140
$85,000	60 Months	$525	$2,273
$90,000	60 Months	$556	$2,407
$95,000	60 Months	$587	$2,541
$100,000	60 Months	$618	$2,674

> **My Tip**
>
> Start slowly with the most essential pieces of equipment and have a plan to introduce other treatments as your business grows. Don't purchase too many pieces of equipment or try to offer too much too soon and run the risk of cash flow problems.

Choosing your products

The products you choose to work with in your salon are very important. This is a key component to your business that needs to be researched and thought out very carefully. It is very difficult to sell something you don't believe in, so choose a product range that you are passionate and enthusiastic about, and that you will be confident working with and recommending to your clients.

Some questions to help you decide:

- How are these products perceived in the market place? Do independent research: read reviews, investigate media coverage or celebrity endorsements, etc.
- Are these products produced by a well-established brand/company, or is this line/range relatively new? Find out how long the product and the company have been in the marketplace.
- What sort of markup do they offer? The higher the markup, the more profit for you.
- Is the range exclusive to salons, or are you competing with retail shops and department stores? This is an

5. Work Smarter, Not Harder!

important consideration. You want clients to come back to you for replacement products and not purchase from somewhere else.

- Is the range available for purchase online from the company or competitors? Once again, you want your clients to purchase from you. If they can easily get their products delivered in one to two days with free shipping, they may choose this option instead of coming to you.
- What sort of support does the company provide for training, marketing materials, product information, etc.? Initial and ongoing training is very important. Ask what they offer.
- What are the opening order requirements? Are they flexible with this? Companies sometimes have minimum quantities or a minimum spend for your first order with them. Collect all your figures and know your obligations before making decisions.
- What are the payment terms? Will they let you have an account, or do products need to be paid for upfront? As I pointed out earlier, it is always best to have an account as this can give you an extra thirty days before you need to pay with your credit card. This means you have the opportunity to sell your products BEFORE you pay for them.
- Will they list you on their website as a stockist and help promote your business? You can potentially pick up a lot of business this way if this service is offered. Make sure you stipulate that you are an appointment-only business on your website and other marketing materials, otherwise you may have customers turning up on your doorstep at any time of the day. A way to prevent this is to only put

your phone number, and not your address, on these listings so that potential customers have to phone you first.

- Are you able to sell this product online, or are there restrictions from the company? Find out if the company have any objections to you selling or promoting the product online through your website or social media pages.

My Tip
Don't limit yourself to just one product range.

Be open to carrying two or three different types of products. One range usually won't suit everyone, so by offering different types of products, you are able to attract and cater for a larger range of clients. You may wish to start with one range initially, and introduce another once you are up and running.

I have three main product ranges in my salon that are all quite different. I like to cater to the different needs of my clients and match each range to their specific concerns.

A big change in the way clients shop for beauty products has taken place since the boom of social media and online shopping. When I started my business, it was easier to sell products in the salon as your clients had very limited options to purchase elsewhere. They would come to you for their treatments, take home their recommended products, and then contact you when they needed to restock. Simple! However one of the secrets to longevity in business is learning to accept that things will constantly change. You must be willing to adapt, embrace change, and work with it rather than stay fixed or rigid in your thinking. Technology is an area that is moving at a phenomenal rate and it has changed the way we do business.

With the addition of shopping carts and PayPal, we can now offer online shopping to our clients and embrace the fact that clients can be purchasing products and treatments from us practically twenty-four hours a day. While we are doing other activities with our families or even sleeping, our business can still be making money!

The secret to getting ahead is getting started

6
Get Equipped

It's time to think about shopping for your entire salon. My advice would be shop around and don't be afraid to ask for discounts. To save money on salon equipment you could enquire if demo models are available or consider purchasing second hand equipment under warranty.

What equipment do you need?
Here is a list of some items you may wish to consider for your setup. I have also included some pricing to use as a guide.

Room

Item	Approximate cost
Stool	$60 – $100
Music player (or use smartphone) Consider subscription to Spotify or Apple Music	$80 upwards $12 per month
Storage (for towels, etc.)	$80 upwards
Trolley	$100 – $300 each IKEA have some great options that are much cheaper than beauty suppliers.
Desk and two seats for consultation/payments	$150 upwards Shop around on eBay, Gumtree, Freedom and Ikea.
Hot towel warmer	$150 - $200
Display cabinet or custom-made shelving to display and store products (Check out IKEA's range)	$200 upwards
Beauty bed	$350 upwards

My Tip
Invest in a really good salon bed.

6. Get Equipped

The salon bed/couch is where the majority of your business will be done, so it is important that your clients are comfortable. You will have people of all sizes and weights, so choosing a sturdy bed that will stand the test of time is worth the investment. It is also very important you can vary the height of your bed for different treatments so you are comfortable when working and not straining which has the potential to cause injuries.

Equipment

Item	Approximate cost
Maggi Lamp (clamp to trolley)	$70
Skin needling device	$1,500 – $2,500 (Cheaper options are available but I have found it is worth investing in the more reputable models)
LED Light Therapy Machine	$7000 upwards (Expect to pay around $14,000 upwards for a device offering a wider range of treatment options)
Microdermabrasion or HydroDermabrasion Machine	$8000 plus (new) You could purchase a demo model at a reduced price or consider purchasing second hand. Search 'Beauty equipment' on Gumtree, eBay and Facebook groups for the hairdressing and beauty industry.

IPL/Laser	$20,000 upwards (new)
	You could enquire about demo models or second hand machines still under warranty. See if training can be included.

Waxing Essentials

Item	Approximate cost
Wooden brow spatulas (Box of 100)	$1
Wooden body spatulas (Box of 100)	$1.50
Wax strips (Box of 100)	$4
Metal applicators	$5
Tweezers	$8 – $20
Aloe vera gel	$10
Pre wax solution	$12
After wax soother	$12
Strip Wax (1L)	$15
Hot wax	$15
Wax citrus cleaner (1L)	$15
Vinyl protective bed cover (Clark Rubber have this on a roll and you can have it cut to size)	$19 per metre
Paper bed roll (35m)	$30
Step stool (for clients to step up on to the bed)	$70
Wax pot (twin)	$100

6. Get Equipped

My Tip
Invest in a sturdy step stool.

A sturdy, stainless steel step stool is a much safer option than the cheap plastic ones. I purchased a good one from Bunnings for around $70 after an incident where a client went straight through the plastic step stool and got her foot stuck. She was okay, thankfully, just a little embarrassed.

Tinting

Eyelash tints (My suggestions – Light Brown, Dark Brown, Black, Blue/Black)	$9 each
Oxidant	$9
Eye protection papers	$6
Kidney dish (plastic)	$3
Glass mixing dish	$3

Facials

Gowns	$30 each
Headbands	$8 each
Protective mats (250 pieces)	$15
Fan brushes for mask	$4
Mask brush – flat	$7
Facial bowls (You can purchase a set of stainless steel mixing bowls)	

Massage oil (1L)	$18
Facial wipes (100 pieces)	$8
Gloves (100 pairs)	$4

General

Alcohol wipes (small individually wrapped wipes, 100 pieces)	$2
Alcohol wipes (tub of 100 pieces)	$6.50

My Tip

Shop for salon supplies such as cotton pads, paper towel and tissues at Aldi or budget supermarkets.

Towels

Hand towels	Buy on sale – try Myer, David Jones, Harris Scarfe, Target etc.
Bath mats (good size for a head towel)	
Large towels	

White towels look fabulous and clean, but they stain very quickly. You will have to spend a lot of money replacing these regularly. Consider this when thinking about the colour scheme for your room. Dark towels are much more practical. For example, if the room has a black and white theme, I would make the head towel, which the client lies on, black rather than white. Also, black headbands last much longer than white ones which tend to stain very quickly.

My Tip

Use a disposable protective mat (barrier pad) on the head towel and replace for each client. This not only looks clean and hygienic for your clients, but it also protects your towels and linen from stains.

Waiting Area

Sofa/seating
Coffee table (for brochures and information about your treatments and any special offers)

Office

Desk and chair
Tablet (for client photos, accounting etc.)
Smartphone
Computer (either desktop or laptop)
Cash tin or cash register
EFTPOS machine/payment facilities

Other

Washing machine (water temperature must be set at 70° Celsius when washing salon items)
Tumble dryer

No matter how you feel, get up, dress up, show up and never give up

7
Believe In Your Brand

It's time to implement the style and feel you would like for your business.

What is branding and why is it important?
Branding is the way your customers perceive you based on the impression you give. Everything that helps your client form an impression of your business is your "brand".

When you think about your branding, think about the experience and feel you want for your clients. Then try to carry that same feeling right through to every element of your business. The style of your salon, marketing materials, website, the way you present yourself, the way you answer the phone, and the way you perform your treatments should all follow a consistent theme.

The first thing to think about is what sort of image you want to create in the salon. Your paint colours, towels, shelving, furniture and other decor all need to reflect the style and mood you wish to create. You might also think about who your ideal client is and what would appeal to them.

An important consideration when deciding upon a colour scheme is the products you will be displaying and retailing. Co-ordinating your colour schemes to best showcase your retail products is very important.

Ultimately, you want your products to appeal to your clients, and colours that blend and compliment these items will help to encourage and boost sales.

My salon branding

My salon branding has changed from when I started. I initially went for a very feminine look, using soft cream paint on the walls, cream towels, and a large piece of cream silk fabric suspended on the ceiling above the treatment bed.

I used burgundy for my logo, with cream and burgundy as my two colours on brochures and business cards. I had a graphic design student design my logo, first brochure, and business cards.

When council regulations changed, I was informed that I needed to install a sink in the room and that it had to contain a hands free tap. Previously I had used the basin directly behind the salon wall in the powder room. As the wall needed to be

7. Believe In Your Brand

repainted after the installation of the new vanity, I decided a whole new look was in order. I had a colour consultant come in to help with a new colour scheme.

I decided on a bolder look, using deep warm tones of green and cream with a bold black/brown painted ceiling. This complimented the dark timber vanity and marble top giving a look that was warm and opulent.

I recently changed the colour scheme and look of the salon once again. This time I painted all the walls white (I used the colour Antique White USA) with one black feature wall.

I painted the timber vanity black and ordered a large French provincial style cabinet from eBay to use as display shelving along one wall. I then followed the black and white theme through with new towels and bedding.

The result was a fresh, clean look achieved with all the white walls. The black shelving and vanity add a touch of drama with a French inspired feeling.

What's your style?

What style are you drawn to? You may want to take into consideration existing factors of your home, such as the exterior style or architecture, as you may choose to continue the same flow or feeling into your salon.

On the following page are a few suggestions that can work well, but use your individuality and choose what compliments the style of your home.

Modern/Minimalistic	Clean, crisp lines, simple neutral colours, metal, glass and steel fittings
Sterile/Medical	Functionality and ultra clean lines using predominantly white colour tones
French/European Inspired	Warm, earthy colours and natural materials like wood and stone
Shabby Chic	Feminine, soft delicate style using white, cream and pastels, and distressed furnishings.
Hollywood Glam	Luxurious, over the top, bold colours and dramatic style that makes a statement

It may be worthwhile to get a paint colour specialist to come out and design a colour scheme for you to help you create the look and feel you want to achieve. Most major paint companies offer this service and sometimes the fee is redeemable off your paint purchase. It may be better to get the right advice upfront rather than make a costly mistake, and be stuck with something that doesn't look right, or have to pay a painter again to change it.

The style you choose will also dictate the style of cabinets or display shelving in your room. There are cost effective, ready-made shelving options available from places like IKEA, or you may opt to have your furniture custom made depending on your budget. Remember you can always upgrade these things later as your business grows. If budget is a concern, start with the cheaper options initially. I change the colour scheme and accessories in my salon every couple of years to

7. Believe In Your Brand

give it a new, fresh look and to keep it interesting for myself and my clients.

You could also look for good purchases for your salon on sites like eBay and Gumtree. You can find new, secondhand, and also factory seconds for furniture and shelving that could potentially save yourself a lot of money. Sometimes, all that is needed is a fresh coat of paint and a little elbow grease to make used furniture look brand new again.

When you decide on your colour scheme and style, continue this theme with your logos, business cards, salon menus and fliers. As mentioned earlier, all of your marketing and branding need to be consistent.

Think about your uniform as well. Choose a colour that compliments your salon. White looks fabulous and fresh, however dark colours like black, brown and navy are much more practical and don't show stains from tints or wax.

Remember, first impressions count. Your aim is to create a mood or feeling that reflects your business, enhances your clients' experience with you, and makes them want to come back. Apart from the visual aspects, another simple way to create a wonderful sensation and feeling is to engage all the senses and, in particular, the sense of smell.

My Tip
Spray the linen and the room with a good quality aromatherapy spray before each client enters the room for their treatment.

Aromatherapy sprays and oils (from flowers and fruits) are known for their healing and therapeutic properties, and are used to enhance a feeling of wellbeing. My clients always comment on how beautiful the salon smells, and how it instantly transforms them into a more relaxed, positive mindset prior to their treatment. Experiment with different fragrances to create different moods and experiences for your clients. Always invest in good quality essential oils and avoid cheap, synthetic oils that may not be good for you to be breathing in on a daily basis. I like Gumleaf essential oils and room sprays from Buckley and Phillips Aromatics (www.buckleyandphillips.com.au).

Himalayan salt lamps are also popular to help purify and improve the quality of the air and also provide a soft, relaxing glow in your room when performing massage or relaxation treatments.

Music also creates a mood or feeling, so be aware of what you are playing in the salon. Clients come to you for an enjoyable experience, and sometimes for relaxation, so choose background music that is appropriate. I use a mix of modern relaxation music, as well as easy listening or classic songs. The radio station Smooth FM puts out some great compilations, and I buy the Mother's Day collection every year. Clients seem to love these and I get lots of positive comments about the choice of music.

The aim of selling is to satisfy a customer need; the aim of marketing is to figure out that need.

8
Stop Selling, Start Helping

One of the key components to successful business and successful selling is to forget about what you need from the other person and start thinking about solving a problem they have. When you approach your business and your clients this way, the sales will take care of themselves. It's all about asking the right questions, listening to your clients to determine what their concerns are, and then finding a solution that works for them. It really is that simple. Don't focus on how much you need to sell or make that week, day or hour. Focus on meeting the needs of your clients by using your skills and knowledge to offer professional advice and solutions.

It's all in the details – the importance of keeping records

One of the most important things you need to do is have systems in place to gather and record as much information and detail as possible about your existing and potential clients – also known as a Customer Relationship Management (CRM) system. This system is your database, which becomes the foundation of your future marketing campaigns.

Building your database

The more information you record, the more specific you can be in targeting your marketing towards meeting the needs of your clients. It is useful to know that it costs about ten times more to attract a new customer than it does to retain an existing one.

I use a manual card system to record client information for those clients who visit the salon and then enter the details into www.mailchimp.com, which I use to design my email campaigns. There are many great systems around that are very simple to use.

How you choose to record your client information is up to you, however you do need to be disciplined and keep your records up to date. Ideally you should update their record as soon as the client has had their treatment, although that's not always possible. So as long as it's completed by the end of the day when your memory is fresh, you won't run the risk of leaving out important details.

You need to be able to add clients manually to your database, and also have a facility that includes an automatic link for clients to add their own details. You can use this on your website or social medial pages. I invite people to join my "VIP list" to receive exclusive special offers and promotions. The more people you have on your database, the more successful your promotions will be and the faster your business will

8. Stop Selling, Start Helping

grow. These people are your target market, and have already either been to see you or shown interest in what you do. Make sure you are consistently keeping them informed of any new treatments, products, or special offers you may have.

Client Records – An absolute must!

Client Consultation Form

Date: _____
Name: _____ Date of Birth: _____
Address: _____
Phone Number: _____ Email: _____
Referred by: _____
What is your main goal for today's treatment? _____

Your Skin Care

1. Have you ever had a facial before? No __ Yes, when? _____
2. Do you have any special skin problems or concerns pertaining to your face or body?
   No __ Yes, please specify _____
3. Do you use Retin-A, AHA or Retinol derivative products?
   No _____ Yes, please specify _____
   Used in the last 3 months? No ___ Yes, how long ago? _____
4. Have you had chemical peels, laser or microdermabrasion? No ____
   Yes, when? _____
5. Have you ever used an acne medicine? No _____ Yes, when? _____
   Which drug? _____
6. What skin care products are you currently using? (List brand where known)
   Face Soap/Cleanser _____ Toner _____
   Day Moisturizer _____ SPF _____
   Exfoliator/Scrub _____ Mask _____
   Eye Product _____ Night Moisturizer _____
   Other _____

7. What areas of concern do you have regarding your Skin: (please check all that apply):

   ☐ Ageing ☐ Pigmentation ☐ Redness ☐ Dryness
   ☐ Breakouts/acne ☐ Blackheads/Whiteheads ☐ Excessive Oil/Shine

8. Please tick other areas you are interested in:

   ☐ Facials ☐ Lash extensions
   ☐ Body ☐ Cosmetic Tattoo
   ☐ Waxing/tinting ☐ Skin Needling
   ☐ Red veins/Capillary removal ☐ IPL (Permanent Hair Removal)
   ☐ Ageing

Step 1: Gathering information of new clients

Have all new clients to the salon fill out a client information sheet. This sheet should contain the client's name, address, phone number(s), date of birth and email address (then add this to your database). It should also ask about the client's medical history or conditions, previous treatments, skincare routine, their current and future skin and beauty concerns, and any other areas of interest.

Step 2: Recording client's details

Record details of the treatment you performed, costs, products purchased and comments about their main concerns and your treatment plan. Also make a note of personal information they share with you during their visit so you can mention it the next time you see them. For example, if a client is going on holidays or has a significant event, ask them how it went. They will appreciate your thoughtfulness and be flattered you remembered details about them. This extra attention to detail helps to build rapport with your clients and makes them feel special. It is also a good way to instigate contact if you haven't heard from them for a while. For example, you can send them a text or message such as:

> *"Hi Jane, was thinking of you and wondered how your holiday in Thailand went? Hope all is good with you, and look forward to seeing you in the salon soon."*

Or,

> *"Hi Jane, hope the wedding went really well. I'm sure you looked absolutely amazing and I would love to see some pictures. Let me know when you would like your next treatment or need to restock your products. I'd love to see you again soon."*

8. Stop Selling, Start Helping

People go where they feel wanted and appreciated, so remember that when dealing with your clients, and let them know you appreciate their business. The personal touches do matter so remember to make your clients feel special.

Step 3: Maintain records

Every time a client visits, you need to update their records to include purchases, treatments performed, progress and any other additional relevant comments.

It is really important to record as much information as possible about your clients' specific skin and beauty concerns. You can obtain a lot of this information in general conversations during the treatment, or you can ask more specific questions about lifestyle, and then share information with them about what you find works. It is your job as a beauty professional to educate your clients about the latest products and treatments available, so make sure you are switched on when clients are with you. Having a lovely, social chat is great and it does build rapport, but you must also make sure you are doing your job, and keeping your clients well informed about what you can offer them.

My Tip
Make sure your client information sheet asks for other areas of concern your client would like to receive information about. Then be sure to follow up and design a package or special offer to suit.

Attracting new clients

Everyone loves a party!

To grow your database and attract new clients, you could consider throwing a "salon opening" celebration. Invite family, friends, neighbours, and perhaps mums from school or ladies you know from your local gym or other associations you belong to. Make an invitation for them and encourage them to bring along a friend. Keep refreshments simple: cake and coffee or drinks and nibbles will suffice. Have some great opening special offers, and have your diary ready to make bookings. Make the offers subject to booking on the day/night of the event, and make it valid for a limited time, perhaps three to four weeks. I would suggest having at least one friend or family member to help you serve refreshments and make bookings, as you will need to mingle and make sure everyone feels comfortable.

Have everyone who attends the event fill out a form so you can add them to your database and include their name, address, email address, and phone number. You could have everyone register on this form as an entry for a "lucky door prize".

You could have take-home goodie bags to say thank you to your guests, and include your salon menu, business card, special offers to use for the following month or two, such as 2-for-1 offers or reward offers for referring a friend. Don't forget to invite them to like and share your social media pages. You could contact your product suppliers and ask if they would like to be involved by contributing product samples, bags, lucky door prizes, or brochures. These same "Open House" ideas work for any other promotions such as Christmas, Mother's Day or Valentine's Day.

Get your details out there – Go local, enlist help

Something I did when I first started my business, which really helped to bring in new local clients, was to have fliers printed with an opening offer or new client offer.

Social media was not so prevalent back then, so much more manual work was required to get my name out there. I took to the streets on foot to hand deliver them into the letterboxes of surrounding houses in my local area. I did so much walking, and the added advantage was that I was doing my exercise at the same time.

I also asked friends who walked if they wouldn't mind dropping some of my fliers in letterboxes around their local area. Other friends were happy to take some fliers and distribute at venues they frequented, such as school and kinder notice boards or coffee shops. I joked that no one was safe visiting me at that time, as they all had to leave with some fliers in hand. I still think letterbox drops in your neighbourhood and surroundings can work effectively when you are starting out. You can hire people to distribute for you, or start with family and friends helping and see if this method works for you. Sometimes you have to be prepared to try different things and see what works best for you.

Get creative about where you could leave your fliers. Brainstorm all the areas your target market may frequent. Some obvious ones where women frequent may be gyms, hairdressers and coffee shops.

Network with other similar businesses

Other similar businesses that offer different treatments from you can be good to network with, and you can refer clients back to each other. Make sure that if you are going to refer someone, you are really comfortable with their level of treatments and service quality, and that you are happy to recommend them to your clients. It will reflect badly on you if someone you personally recommend isn't a professional operator like yourself, and may leave your client questioning your judgement. I have a close girlfriend who is a hairdresser. She also works from home and we have successfully referred clients between the two of us for many years. As we are friends, and have a similar style and way of doing business, we find it works really well and we attract the same type of clientele.

Local businesses

Your local doctor, dentist, physiotherapist or other healthcare professionals may be happy to let you leave some fliers in their waiting room or notice board. You can only ask and my favourite saying is "nothing ventured, nothing gained". If you want to succeed in your business, you need to take some risks and step out of your comfort zone. The worst scenario that can happen is they say no. No big deal, just say you understand and thanks anyway. If you don't ask, you could miss out on a potential client picking up your flier from that business and making their first booking with you.

Local paper

You could contact your local paper and consider placing some advertisements. Generally they advise that a level of consistency with your advertising works best if you have ads going in their paper every week for a period of time. It is worth asking if they would be willing to give you some free or discounted editorial space to help promote your new business.

Join professional organisations

It is a good idea to belong to professional associations relevant to your business. You can advertise that you are a member of these associations which can help build your credibility with potential clients. Find out how the organisation can help you with your business. They sometimes advertise member details online for potential clients to contact and may also offer training and networking events for free or for discounted rates for their members. Take a look at:

- Professional Beauty – www.professionalbeauty.com.au
- Aesthetics Advisory Network (APAN) – https://apanetwork.com
- Association of Professional Aestheticians of Australia (APAA) – https://apaa.com.au

Referrals – There for the asking

A great way to double your bookings is to ask each client who comes to you to refer someone else. You can do this by handing them a card for a special offer or discount to pass on to a friend. You then let them know that they will both receive the same offer, or personalise a special promotion for them if you know there is a particular treatment they would like to have as a thank you for sending someone else your way.

2-for-1 offers

A good way to introduce new clients into your business is to offer a 2-for-1 deal. This works particularly well at Christmas or Mother's Day when people are looking for gifts. They purchase one treatment for a friend (which can be a gift voucher) and receive a second one free of charge or 50% off to use for themselves. Make some terms and conditions to this offer, such as that both treatments must be used by a particular date. Perhaps allow one month maximum, as you want them to book in soon. The whole idea of the promotion is to boost your short term bookings. This is also a good offer to run during quiet times when you need to fill up your appointment book. The other thing worth noting about gift vouchers is that a certain percentage are never redeemed, therefore you are basically receiving "money for nothing".

Package offers

Package offers which include value added treatments or discounts are a great way to reward your clients who commit to a course of treatments. I offer a discount or add extra products or services for packages of three or six treatments prepaid in advance. You could also introduce a "Pay 3 and get 1 free" option which works equally well. Experiment with different options to see which one your clients prefer. The benefits are that you have a lump sum paid upfront, which is great for cash flow, and it also means your client is committed to continuing their visits with you. Otherwise, they may have every intention of having regular treatments with you, but then life gets in the way! They have a medical expense, or a vet bill, or the car needs servicing, and they prioritise other things instead. If they have a prepaid package, they have already paid for the service and are more likely to keep their appointments. They may also need to stock up on their products, and as they will be in regularly they will be exposed to current promotions, new products, and impulse items (such as lipsticks, mascaras, etc.). A lot of my clients visit regularly on a two weeks basis, and they continually repeat their packages as they expire.

Payment plans

Another way to ensure repeat business from your clients is to offer a payment plan for your packages. This means that you process their credit card at agreed intervals while they continue to have their treatments with you, until the package is paid off. For example: for a package of treatments valued at $800, they may be happy to pay $200 upfront and then allow you to deduct $200 from their account every two weeks for three further payments. You keep their credit card details on file, and make the payments yourself on their behalf. I would advise having a form for your client to fill out agreeing to these terms and authorising you to do so on their behalf. Include the dates the payments will be made, then keep a copy for yourself and print one for the customer as well. There are also organisations who can organise this on your behalf for a small fee. You could also look into Ezypay or similar systems that allow the customer to purchase their goods and pay later whilst you get paid upfront.

Newsletters, blogs and promos

Set up a newsletter system and send regular promotions to the clients on your database. MailChimp is free and reasonably easy to use, and there are other options you could choose from. Try and send regular newsletters (perhaps monthly) and relevant promotions, however don't overdo it.

My Tip
Don't reinvent the wheel. Use the promotional materials prepared and supplied by the companies you deal with for your promotions.

These are usually pre-made and ready to use for your social media and email campaigns. If you need to personalise your campaigns for a specific offer, ask if the company's marketing department would be willing to help. They are usually more than happy to assist and not only does this save you time, but your campaigns would look professional.

Invite the clients on your database to follow you on social media by providing the links to your pages on Facebook,

Instagram, and other platforms. Post relevant content and information on these platforms to keep your clients up to date. This is a great place to post "before and after" pictures of clients (always check for permission with the client first) as people love real pictures and stories. Invite your clients to put reviews up on Facebook and Google if they are happy with your service. A lot of potential clients read reviews and comments. In fact, I read that in 2014, 88% of consumers read online reviews and 72% of them trust online reviews[1] when considering a business. Positive reviews can also help your rankings with Google which may allow your business to show up higher in searches.

Giveaways

Competitions and giveaways are an excellent way to encourage interaction and exposure for your business.

Here are some basic ideas that you could try yourself:

Facebook competition – Example

Win a Salon Treatment Voucher valued at $150 plus a take home skincare box valued at $123

How to Enter:

"Like" this page

"Tag" a friend

"Share" this post

---

1. BrightLocal 2014, 'Local Consumer Review Survey, 2014', <www.brightlocal.com/wp-content/uploads/2014/07/Local-Consumer-Review-Survey-20141.pdf>

8. Stop Selling, Start Helping

Conditions: You can enter as many times as you like. Complete steps 1, 2 and 3 and then each time you "tag" a friend it counts as an entry. The winner is the one who tags the most friends. Entries close this Friday.

Variations to try:

- Feature a "Product of the Month". Include a picture of the product and a short blurb about its benefits. Offer one as a giveaway and invite your audience to "tell us in 25 words or less why you would like to win this prize".
- Feature a "Product of the Month". Offer one as a prize for the person who writes the best review of that product.
- Offer a FREE Treatment as a prize and invite your audience to "tell us in 25 words or fewer why you would benefit from one".

My Tip

Announce your winner and then contact everyone else who entered and offer them a special promotion as a consolation prize.

Use treatments as prizes as they cost you only your time. Also, offering a treatment as a prize potentially brings a new client into the salon who may purchase future treatments and packages.

Another way to keep costs down for your promotions is by using products you get as "freebies" or special offers from company promotions as your prizes.

Loyalty programs

These can work really well to help clients feel they are a "VIP" or "special" member of your business and that they will be rewarded for their loyalty. You could run special promotions that are only available to your VIP clients or have a system where they earn points towards free treatments and products. This encourages repeat business and if it is calculated on how much they spend with you they will be more motivated to purchase their products from you when they need to restock.

Salon promotions

There are two major events every year that offer a massive opportunity for your business: Christmas and Mother's Day. We have a huge advantage in our industry, as beauty treatments and products rate very highly as popular gifts for women. It is absolutely worth taking the time to prepare in advance for your promotional activities over these periods.

The joy of Christmas

Christmas is the most lucrative time for the retail industry and it is important to be organised and capitalise on this to the fullest. Below is an example of an event I have had success with that you may like to try:

Hold a VIP Christmas Open House

Invite clients and friends to attend an exclusive shopping event.

On the opposite page is a sample invitation I have used previously:

8. Stop Selling, Start Helping

You and a friend are invited to the

Envisage Beauty

V.I.P. Christmas Open House

Wednesday 2nd December
Open House from 10am – 7pm

- You will be presented with your free goodie bag on arrival
- You will be served Champagne, Tea, Coffee and nibbles
- You will be eligible for loads of fantastic Lucky Door Prizes
- Plus Huge discounts and savings on the day
- Exclusive Gift Voucher offers
- Surprise special offers

Come join in the fun!
RSVP: 25th November to Jo 0407716686

This invitation only event is exclusively for Envisage Clients and their guests. Unfortunately due to space limitations on the day we are unable to accommodate children.

Contact your skincare and beauty suppliers and see if they would like to be involved on the day to help promote their ranges, perform demonstrations, talk to clients and help with sales. Also ask if they would be willing to contribute samples, products or brochures to use for goodie bags and lucky door prizes.

Mother's Day

Mother's Day is also a peak selling time for our industry. Gift vouchers are really popular at this time so you could start your voucher campaign at least a month before and perhaps have a different offer each week leading up to the day. Email out to your database and be sure to include your offers on your social media sites.

I have found combination offers work well. For example, you could do a gift voucher for a relaxation facial with a take home product or gift box and package them together. Be sure to advertise that you also do gift vouchers for dollar amounts that allows the recipient to choose how she would like to spend it. Perhaps you could add an extra amount as an incentive such as for every $50 spent you will add a bonus $10 to the voucher.

If you are smart with your promotions for these two major events and focus your efforts on selling gift vouchers and packages, you can ensure a steady flow of business for the entire year.

It is a good idea to always have at least one promotion running in the salon. I usually have a sign promoting it on the front counter or in a prominent position. You can also email the same promotion out to your client database.

Valentine's Day

You could focus on a Valentine's Day promotion and target men looking for gift ideas for their partners. Men love gifts which are easy to buy such as gift vouchers or pre-wrapped gift sets. You may like to try adding in some chocolate hearts or champagne into your gift packs. It's your chance to get creative and see what works.

My Tip

Keep it as simple as possible for the guys. Most men like their shopping experiences to be as quick and painless as possible. Have three choices of gift voucher price points or product gift sets and let them choose. The middle or top price point is usually the most popular.

Examples of Additional Promotions To Try

- Join the draw to win a skincare pack when you purchase a gift voucher.
- Receive a FREE $50 salon treatment voucher when you spend over $200 on gift packs.
- Have a tiered offer such as "Spend $100 get a FREE $20 Voucher", "Spend $200 get a FREE $50 Voucher", "Spend over $450 and get a FREE $100 Voucher".
- Offer a free product sample pack with every gift voucher purchased. You could wrap these in clear cellophane bags with ribbons (a variety of sizes of bags and ribbons are available from two dollar shops at really cheap prices). Have these on display in the salon next to your gift vouchers and have a sign highlighting the offer.

Example of card I use to encourage waxing or cosmetic tattoo clients to try a facial treatment:

Thankyou

For choosing Envisage Beauty for your Skincare and Beauty needs. To show our appreciation, I would like to offer you the opportunity to try one of our other popular Treatments at 50% off the regular price. Treatments Include: Microdermabrasion, Skin Peels, Oxygen Treatments, Skin Needling, IPL permanent hair reduction, IPL Skin Rejuvenation (brown spot, red vein removal and collagen stimulation).

FOR MORE INFORMATION ABOUT OUR TREATMENTS, VISIT OUR WEBSITE: envisagebeauty.com.au and join our VIP MAILING LIST to receive your newsletters and VIP exclusive offers!

FOLLOW US ON FACEBOOK & INSTAGRAM

Once again, a big Welcome to Envisage Beauty.
Kind Regards,
Jo McKenzie

Offer Valid for one Month.

8. Stop Selling, Start Helping

Example of card I send to clients I haven't seen for a while:

Would Love to See You!

I have lots of new and exciting services and products to tell you about! Please accept with my compliments $50 off the Treatment of your choice and 10% off products for your next visit. All you need to do to take advantage of your offer is book within the next month. Treatments Include: Microdermabrasion, Skin Peel, Skin Needling, Oxygen Treatment, IPL permanent hair reduction, IPL Skin Rejuvenation (brown spot, red vein removal and collagen stimulation).

FOR MORE INFORMATION ABOUT OUR TREATMENTS, VISIT OUR WEBSITE: envisagebeauty.com.au and join our VIP MAILING LIST to receive your newsletters and VIP exclusive offers!

FOLLOW US ON FACEBOOK & INSTAGRAM

I look forward to catching up again soon.
Kind Regards,
Jo McKenzie   *Offer Valid for one Month.*

Your smile is your logo, your personality is your business card, how you leave others feeling after an experience with you becomes your trademark

9
My Secret Planning Tips for Success

Find the balance

One of the most difficult things to overcome when you decide to work for yourself at home is managing your time and being able to separate work time and home time. There can be a temptation to keep working all the time. For example, there is always something to do, be it marketing or book work, and it can be hard to shut off from that mode of work, work, and work. Finding a good balance between business and personal life is really important. Looking after your health and wellbeing is also crucial, as making time for exercise and time out helps you to stay fit, well, and more productive in your business.

The other extreme you may experience is that you get so distracted by the home environment that you don't keep up with the tasks you need to do for your business. For example, you think you will spend some time doing your marketing, but a friend wants to call in for coffee. Or you notice the house looking a bit messy, so you clean up instead, then put the washing away, then prepare dinner, and before you know it, your day has gone and the marketing still hasn't been done.

Plan your time

The only way to find that balance and discipline is by prioritising and planning ahead how you wish to distribute your time. Get yourself a good diary with plenty of room to write all your appointments and tasks in. You can get special appointment diaries from salon suppliers. I use the Collins desk diary/planner A4 size from my local newsagent, which has one day to each page, allowing plenty of room to write everything in.

Think about what days you would like to work in your salon. It is best to try and book your clients in "tight", which means either full days or blocks where you see clients one after the other, rather than having your appointments all over the place where you stop and start. It is much more productive to have set salon days and times, leaving other time slots free. You can then schedule time for other tasks such as paying bills, book work, marketing, stock orders, research and training. Running a successful salon is not just about performing treatments and selling products to clients in the room (although this needs to be the highest priority, as this is where your income comes from). You will find there are quite a few other tasks you need to stay up to date and on top of. If you don't make time for these on a regular basis, you will not be organised and run the risk of becoming stressed and overwhelmed trying to keep up with everything. The more disciplined you can be with your time, the smoother and more efficient your business will run. One of my favourite sayings is "people don't plan to fail, they just fail to plan".

Make good impressions

Write all your commitments as they come up into your salon diary. This includes all personal appointments, obligations, exercise classes, and doctors appointments. Be aware that clients may see your diary and can sometimes read what is on your pages.

With that in mind, think about how you write things in your diary and how they will appear to clients. For example, if you are meeting a friend and you wish to block that time out in your diary, instead of writing "lunch" or the name of the restaurant, put your friend's name in and cross out the necessary time frame, just as you would for a salon booking. When you open your diary to make a booking for a client, and they see lots of appointments booked in, they get the impression you are someone who is successful and in demand.

You may need to develop some codes that only you understand and know what they are. Nothing is more offputting to clients than seeing an empty appointment diary, especially when you are asking them to rebook with you. How would you feel? Would you be keen to book in with someone that no one else seemed to be booking with, or would you prefer to book with someone who is in high demand? You need to appear busy and successful so people will want to do business with you. It really is that simple. Even if you don't have many client bookings when you start out or have a quiet week with bookings, if you have some other appointments or commitments pencilled in, it certainly looks better to clients. Be aware of how they perceive you and your business. There is a great saying, nothing succeeds like success! I love this saying and it is so true. We all want to do work with someone who is busy and in demand. It's human nature, so be aware of how you are coming across and the impressions you give.

Be positive and grateful

The same applies when clients ask if you are busy, which is a general conversation question that you will get asked many times. I always reply, "Yes, I'm flat out which is great". This reinforces to them that I am in demand and that they are working with someone that lots of other people want to see as well. Also by saying it is wonderful to be busy, I am letting them know I am happy and thankful for their business.

Your attitude is a very important part of your clients' experience with you. Never complain to clients about being busy. Even if you are exhausted or feeling overwhelmed, you must show your clients that you appreciate their business. People go where they feel wanted. Let me say this very important sentence again: PEOPLE GO WHERE THEY FEEL WANTED. Remember to be grateful for every client that chooses to walk through your door. Show them that you appreciate their business by being positive and making their experience with you a rewarding and uplifting one that they look forward to coming back for.

My Tip

Never complain about being busy. Whatever you put out there in your thoughts and words will be reflected back. If you are grateful and thankful for every client who chooses to come to you, you will have more clients to be grateful and thankful for.

Insist others respect your time

One of the challenges you may find is getting family and friends to take your business seriously and respect your work time. Some people think that because you work from home, you are readily available and accessible if they need you. You need to be firm that you are working and not available during scheduled work time. If necessary, let them know what time you are available to visit or chat and they will see that you are taking your business seriously and learn to respect that. It is important to be strict with your work time and not allow others to dictate how you spend your time. This time is important for completing the tasks you need to do in order to run your business successfully. If you don't take it seriously, no one else will.

Get family on board

The other important part to being professional and disciplined in your home business is to have family members co-operating and on board. They must understand and respect that people are paying you for a service and that you need to present a professional image at all times. You will need to educate family members about what is expected if they are home when you have clients in your salon.

A funny story comes to mind as to why we had to make one particular rule in our home. The powder room and toilet is directly behind the salon wall. One day in the middle of my relaxation facial massage with my client, I heard my son open the toilet door, lift the lid and, well, you can guess the rest …

I was holding my breath as we could hear him peeing right in the middle of a beautiful relaxing massage. This was followed by the sound of the toilet flushing, the tap being turned on before he loudly pushed the door shut and went on his way. Talk about a mood buster! As we have three toilets in our house, the rule from then on became "use one of the other toilets in the house (quietly!) when I have a client with me". You may need to adapt this one to suit your facilities, but let family members know they need to be as quiet as possible when you have someone with you.

The same goes for talking and walking around the house while you have someone in the salon with you. Ask family members to be mindful of noise and remind them that you need to provide a quiet and professional environment for your customers at all times. My kids know never to interrupt me while I am in the salon. Our joke was "unless your head is hanging off, do not interrupt me when I am with a client".

You may need some kind of system that informs everyone in the house that you have a client with you. Perhaps a sign on your door that states "treatment in progress" or something similar that lets family members know. We had a few mishaps over the years simply because my kids didn't realise I was with someone in the salon. They have called out to me or yelled at each other (sibling rivalry!) while the client and I could hear everything. I have had to excuse myself and get their attention and alert them to the fact I have someone with me. They were always very apologetic and red faced when they realised.

9. My Secret Planning Tips for Success

No distractions

If you have younger children, I would advise having someone looking after them in another part of the house to keep them safe and to ensure you are not being interrupted whilst you are working. If you are distracted and worried about them instead of concentrating on your work, trust me, the client will pick up on this and you run the risk he/she may not come back.

No Pets

The same goes for our pets. As much as we love them and no matter how cute they are, it is never appropriate to let them wander around freely when you have clients with you. Put them outside or keep them confined in another room when you are working. Apart from the fact some people may not appreciate your pets being around, it is also an issue of hygiene. Keep in mind also that some people could be allergic to your pets. You are performing treatments that require the utmost cleanliness and a salon environment is not the place for pets. You could have problems with the health department as well if a client lodged a complaint.

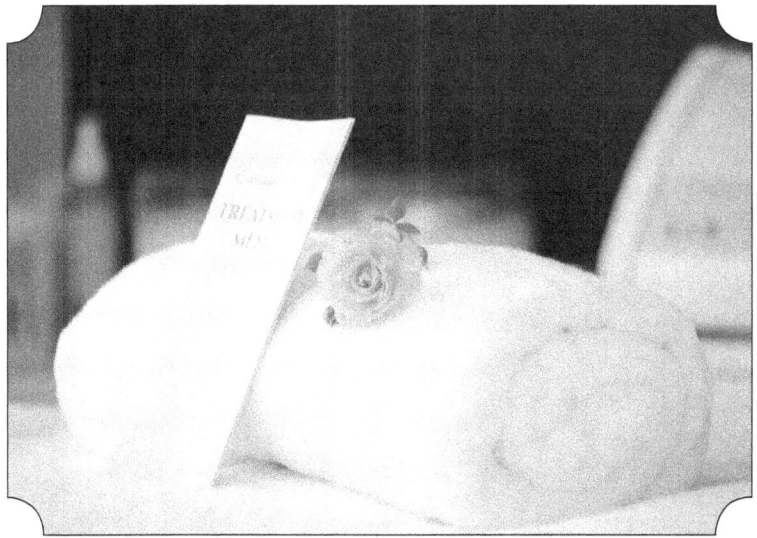

Every journey begins with a single step

Afterword

Congratulations on reaching the end of this book. I hope you feel motivated, confident and inspired to begin your journey as a business owner and that you look forward to opening your very own professional home salon.

We work in the most amazing industry, where we have the opportunity to make people look and feel good about themselves. Embrace and enjoy what a privilege that is.

I look forward to hearing from you and receiving updates on your progress. If you have any questions about anything I haven't covered or you would like more information, please feel free to send me an email.

I wish you success, prosperity and happiness. Stay focused, be passionate, dream big but most of all, have fun and enjoy your journey!

Lots of love,

Jo
xxxxx

Acknowledgements

To the team at Busybird publishing and in particular, my publisher Blaise van Hecke. Thank you for your patience, humour, warmth and encouragement. You have made the process of writing my first book so enjoyable and rewarding and have allowed me to turn a dream into a reality. To Kev Howlett, thanks for your professionalism and attention to detail and for making our photo shoot fun.

To the ladies who have been clients at "Envisage Beauty", many who I also consider as friends, thank you for your support and loyalty over the years. Thank you for not just allowing me the privilege of looking after your skin and beauty needs, but for sharing and trusting me with so many of your personal stories.

To my wonderful family and friends whose love and support means the world. Thank you.

About The Author

Jo McKenzie grew up in Bendigo, a country town in Victoria. She now lives in the eastern suburbs of Melbourne with her two children.

After graduating from high school she worked in an accounting firm before securing a position in the tourism industry where she worked for the next seven years.

Her involvement and passion for the beauty industry started when she decided to become a party plan consultant, selling skin care and makeup as a part time hobby. She excelled in this area, winning many awards and prizes along the way. It was through this that she realised she had a gift for sharing and teaching her passion for skincare and makeup.

She moved to Melbourne to pursue her career and completed her Diploma of Beauty Therapy in 1992. She worked in leading salons around Melbourne before opening her own professional clinic "Envisage Beauty" from home in 2002. She has continued her education over the years and is highly qualified in many advanced skincare and beauty treatments. She specialises in age management and skin rejuvenation with the use of combined therapies such as collagen induction therapy (skin needling), microdermabrasion, hydrodermabrasion, sonophoresis, oxygen treatments and chemical skin peels. She holds a current Intense Pulse Light (IPL)/Laser Safety Officers certificate and is an IPL/Laser skin specialist. Jo is also an experienced cosmetic tattooist and micro blade artist who has been passionate about creating natural looking semi permanent makeup enhancements for her clients since obtaining this qualification in 2007.

Jo is well known and well respected in the beauty industry for her professionalism and knowledge as a skin and beauty specialist, and for her longevity and adaptability as a salon owner and businesswoman.

Offers

FREE additional salon tips and tricks

Join our VIP Members list to receive updates on future programs and additional marketing information to use for your business.

To join, submit your details by email.

Like to experience a Treatment with this industry professional?

SAVE 50% off the Facial treatment of your choice and use this opportunity to have all your skin and beauty questions answered by Jo.

To redeem, submit your details by email or text and mention this offer.

Free phone coaching session (Valued at $199)

Talk with Jo in a free phone strategy session to answer all your questions about how to achieve your beauty or business goals.

One-to-one mentoring

Want to work with Jo to help you set up your business for success?

Would you like to know how to revamp your existing beauty business?

Enquire about our personal mentoring programs and salon set up packages.

To redeem offers:

> **Email**: jo@envisagebeauty.com.au
> **Text**: 04 0771 6686
> **Call**: 03 9876 4432
> **Website**: www.envisagebeauty.com.au
> **Instagram**: @envisagebeauty1
> **Facebook**: Envisage Beauty – Ringwood North

Bonus Interview

with Lourbuen Perez-Vergamalis: Director/Clinical Educator – Complexion Group

Tell me a little about your background and how you became involved in the beauty industry.

I was an accountant for fifteen years, so I had a strong background in the financial side of running and operating a business. My journey in the beauty industry is a very personal one, having had very bad acne myself and continually trying treatments and products to help my condition. I found going to dermatologists were expensive and too clinical, whilst some of the beauty salons were too spa/relaxation orientated rather than offering results.

I decided to pursue my personal interest in the beauty industry and decided a career change was in order. I wanted to offer clinical treatments that were results driven but still offered some pampering and relaxation.

I started with my Diploma of Beauty Therapy and then went on to complete my Advanced Diploma of Cosmetic Dermal Science, and also gained my qualification as a Dermal Therapist Trainer and Educator.

I am a registered member and educator of Aesthetics Practitioners Advisory Network (APAN).

I started my practice by renting a consulting room in a medical clinic in the eastern suburbs of Melbourne using all modalities that I learnt from school which includes IPL, LED and PDT, RF, Skin Peel, Skin Needling and LASER for hair reduction, rejuvenation and tattoo removal. The whole experience gave me a good knowledge on what treatment brings regular clients, what equipment is a must have, what works well, what skin care product works for the business and for the client, and most important is what training and support the therapist and the owner needs to operate the machine they purchased and the pre/post care treatment.

I then decided to move to a bigger place and open a complexion clinic and training centre in Blackburn. We operate as a fully functional treatment clinic focusing on skin and age management and also offer a training centre and equipment supply service for people in the beauty industry.

My objective in life is "be a blessing to everyone around me". I consider everyone I deal with in business as my family and only aim to bless them all. This includes honesty, genuine care, and support.

What are the most popular treatments with your clients?

The most popular treatments would be anti-ageing treatments for reduction of lines and wrinkles, pigmentation, and facial vascular treatments. We normally use a combined treatment of Skin Peel, Dermabrasion and LASER. But some clients need an instant result so we move them to injectables which includes vitamin infusion, fillers, wrinkle relaxer, platelet-rich plasma (PRP), and stem cells. This is followed closely by acne management and post acne scarring and post inflammatory hyperpigmentation (PIHP) treatments. Body treatments such as fat cavitation for contouring and cellulite are gaining popularity as well.

Which would you say are most essential pieces of equipment to have in a salon and why?

Definitely a microdermabrasion or hydrodermabrasion machine, collagen induction therapy (CIT)Pen, and LED light device. This combination of equipment can treat and improve skin conditions including acne, pigmentation, scarring, and skin rejuvenation in general.

Which other treatments would you add?

Chemical peels and oxygen jet spray for solution infusion. And a proper home care pre and post treatment with their CIT roller is a must-have for a better result.

If you had to work with a really tight budget which piece of equipment would be your number one choice for offering the most treatment options?

I would say the Hydromax. This is a combination of hydrodermabrasion and oxygen jet spray.

Which piece of equipment offers the best return on investment?

I would say the LED machine and the CIT Pen. Treatment for skin needling is from $199-350 and your repayment is roughly $70 per week. The LED machine is like your machine therapist where you can leave it on while working on the next client.

Would you suggest buying or leasing your equipment when you are first starting up?

Most people starting out have a fairly limited budget. I would always advise leasing your equipment to avoid cash flow problems. As an example, for just over $100 per week or around $500 per month you can lease some key equipment pieces to enable you to do a variety of treatments and you can claim the whole amount as a tax deduction.

Reliability of equipment is very important in a salon. Anything to look out for when purchasing equipment?

Yes, definitely a big factor to look at and consider highly because I have been a victim of this. Ensure that the trainer is at least a qualified dermal therapist who can train you effectively and understands the clinical side rather than someone who is just qualified to sell equipment. Also, make sure you see and test the machine because it is a large investment to start with. Furthermore, check with previous customers for their experience of support. Make sure someone from the company will be easily accessible to help you with questions and queries about your equipment and clinical enquiries. In the event of malfunctions, you need backup support to come out and fix or collect your machine and return it to you as soon as possible or provide you with a temporary replacement.

What advice would you give someone opening a clinic?

Do not rush. Do not contact any sales agent yet as they will sell everything to you and you will get so confused. Try to connect to people in your industry and check their opinion. Don't try and buy every piece of equipment first up. Unless you have a very healthy budget to start up with, grow with your business and maybe look at introducing one new piece of equipment each year rather than all at once.

What mistakes have you made or do you see in this industry and how would you avoid them?

Work with a coach or mentor in the industry. Someone with experience in the industry can save you a lot of wasted time and money by helping you to set up properly and put you on the right path. You need support from someone who has done it, otherwise you end up feeling stressed and frustrated when things go wrong.

What qualifications and training would you recommend for someone wanting to work for themselves at home?

For younger people, I would usually recommend Diploma of Beauty Therapy would be a minimum qualification. For someone of mature age who has had experience in the workplace perhaps in a managerial role or who has some business experience, then possibly Cert IV would suffice initially. It is always good to keep learning and adding to your qualifications though so I would always encourage someone to continue their studies, perhaps on a part time basis, whilst starting their business. As I mentioned above, a coach or mentor would be essential particularly for someone with little or no business experience or previous beauty therapy experience.

How did you attract new clients into your business?

Majority comes from word of mouth. However, in an attempt to broaden our client reach and gain more exposure, we tried working with Groupon. It has been quite successful for us. At least 70% of these clients become our regular clients for packages and injectables. The biggest mistake on using deals and heavily discounted promotions is if you have nothing more to upsell. If you just focus on giving cheap discount offers without upselling or obtaining future bookings, then these adverts are not worth your time at all.

Bonus Interview

with Tania De Vincentis: Owner – "Designing Hair" home business, Mooroolbark

I first met Tania in 2001 when I started working at a local salon which offered hair and beauty treatments. She had been working as a senior hairstylist there and I joined the company to look after the Beauty Salon. About twelve months later, the salon closed overnight, going into receivership and staff were advised by text that they no longer had jobs and not to come in the next day. At this stage I had already started my salon from home on a part time basis which had been running for about four months. I saw this as a sign to put my efforts into my own business and concentrate my efforts full time on building this up.

Tania was understandably shocked to lose her job so suddenly. I said to her "why don't you open up from home and work for yourself?" It was not something she had ever considered in the past. I offered to help her as I had recently set up my own salon from home. I told her to seriously consider starting her own business as she was an experienced hair stylist who was passing on all her profits and talent to someone else.

Tell me a little about your background and when you started your hairdressing career?

I went from high school straight into hairdressing college. After completing my course I worked at various salons in Melbourne and also worked as a mobile hairdresser for a couple of years. At one point I wanted a change from hairdressing and tried office work but soon realised I missed the interaction with clients and that I actually loved the creativity hairdressing allowed.

How did you feel when I suggested you open your own business and work for yourself?

At first I thought "What do I do? How do I get started?" It all seemed a little overwhelming but talking with you helped me to feel more confident. The fact that you had already been through the process of setting yours up, and that I had someone to help me, did make a big difference. I decided I had nothing to lose by giving it a go and I am so glad I did.

What concerns did you have about opening your own business from home?

Probably the main concerns were "How do I attract clients?" and "Will I be able to get enough clients to earn a reasonable income?"

Bonus Interview: Tania De Vincentis

How did you attract clients initially to get your business started?

I put an ad in the local paper for four weeks running and was blown away with the response. I had won a hairdressing award around that time, so I made mention of that in the ad. I included a headshot of me and an opening offer for clients responding to the ad. It was that simple! I had many calls and bookings in response to the ad and my business was up and running.

What has been the advantages of working for yourself in a home business?

The flexibility has been a blessing. I have a husband and two sons so just being able to work around school, sport and family commitments has been wonderful. When the boys were younger I was able to be here when they got home from school and also just being able to organise dinner or chores in between clients helped tremendously.

What advice would you give to someone wanting to work from home like you?

Be careful not to burn out! Manage your time and appointments wisely. When I started I worked some really long hours but I learnt that it takes a toll on your body. You need to allow proper break times to rest, eat, exercise, etc.

How do you think clients see a home based business in comparison to a shop salon situation?

It depends a lot on how you choose to run your business. If you are professional and run a business that is clean and well presented, and you are good at what you do, I have found a lot of clients prefer the more personal home setting. They can park freely, they have my complete attention for their entire appointment time, and they have consistency as well.

Having said that, if I do have a potential client call up and assume that my prices may be "cheap" or that I offer "budget" treatments, I explain that I am an experienced stylist who specialises in quality customised treatments using high quality products. I have found if these clients do decide to give you a try, they are so happy with the result and the comments they receive from others, that they can turn into a long term loyal client.

I would say if you are thinking about running your own home based salon then you should go for it! Enlist the help of someone who knows all the shortcuts to success which will save you time and money and then just focus on what you do best.

All the best!

Welcome to Envisage Beauty

Client enjoying a treatment

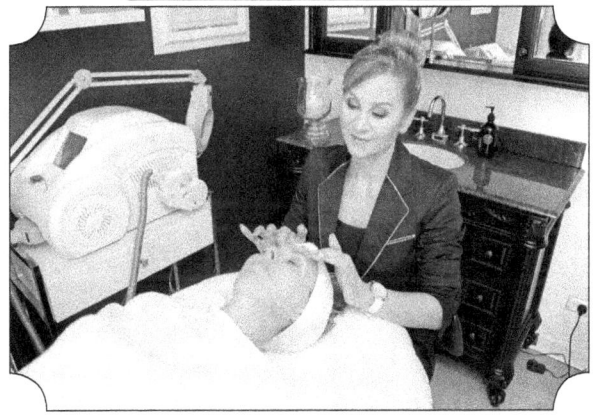

Salon 2018

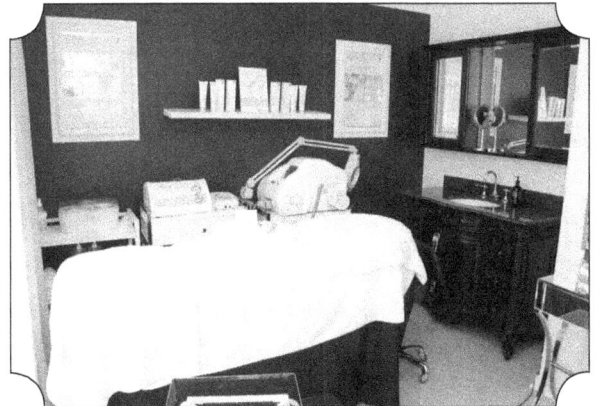

Salon shelving unit 2018

Salon 2013 - 2017

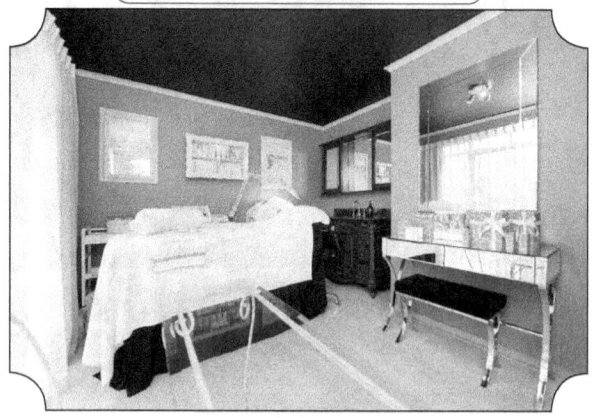

Salon 2013 – 2017

www.ingramcontent.com/pod-product-compliance
Lightning Source LLC
Chambersburg PA
CBHW070951080526
44587CB00015B/2261